Inspirations—Dreams and Love

I hope you enjoy have to
some I wrote love to you
say

love
Carol

Inspirations—Dreams and Love

Gene Augustine

To order additional copies of this book, contact:
Xlibris Corporation
1-888-795-4274
www.Xlibris.com
Orders@Xlibris.com
98080

Contents

My Wife Belle

(Born: 9/12/1938, passed away 6/17/2010)

My Inspiration

The many things you inspired in me
Are in this book for you to see.
My thoughts and dreams,
My memories too.
How much we cared and the moments
We shared,
What all we done and have yet to do,
And all the love I hold for you.

-Gene Augustine

POEMS

By Gene Augustine

Me

Let me see what I would be
If I'd start over at the age of three,
Astronaut, Explorer, politician who's free
All tough choices for a child who's three
But if I could start over at the age of three
I think I'd just like to be me.

Love

Love is more then just a word
Not one just read, not one just heard.
Its something felt way deep inside
With one you laughed,
With one you cried.
An emptiness when she's not near
The one you hold so very dear.

Beyond

What lies beyond what we can see?
Are we all we are or need to be
If we stay the same, try not to gain
What we are now we will remain.
We must push on, we must improve,
Our minds must find some higher groove.
We can't accept what now we know
For if we do we cease to grow.

Yesterday

Does yesterday go away forever?
Or can we keep and bring it back whenever.
Does time have banks from which we borrow?
Does midnight end today or start tomorrow.

Hearts

Can this be true,
What I have felt you feel it too.
Those feelings I have held so long,
Now to us both they do belong.
The love I've held in my heart for you,
Does not belong to one but two.
If this be so, our hearts have won,
Now together, not two—but one.

Go together

Sugar cubes and coffee,
Ice cream and apple pie.
Sun and a clear sky,
Stars and the night sky.
John Wayne and western movies,
Trick or treat and Halloween,
Santa Claus and Christmas,
Betwixt and between.
I suppose you are wondering
What this is leading to.
Well—each goes with the other,
As I go with you.

Let Me

Let me caress and softly hold;
The thoughts and words to me you told,
Let me always feel your love, my dear
Let your laughter ring forever in my ear.
Let me always think thoughts I do now
Let us be together someplace, somehow.
We both know how much we care,
Let it grow forever. this love we share.

Linger Long

Linger long these thoughts of you,
Forever stay with me.
Linger long these words I hear,
Happy they have made me be.
Linger long these feelings felt,
Within my heart and soul.
Linger long this love for you,
That forever will I hold.
Linger long my shining star,
Linger long.

Don't change

I want, I need
You as you are.
To have to hold
In futures far.
Please don't change
The things you do.
For I love the whole,
Not part of you.

You

If I count
My thoughts,
My desires,
The memories of you,
I keep within.
You are with me
In all I do.

Faces

As you are walking
On some crowded street,
Carefully look at the faces you meet.
Some will be wrinkled,
Some will look old,
Some will be sad,
Some will look cold.
Some will be happy,
Carefree and gay.
Some will be smiling,
Just make your whole day.
So each day you're walking,
Take heed as you do.
For someone is watching,
The faces on you.

My Friend

My friend and dear old buddy,
I sure am missing you,
I also know the man you were,
That others miss you too.
You left us way too sudden,
We had miles left to go,
There are still a many golf course,
We had yet to know.
I know you will be listening,
For help in what I do,
And for those times I'll whisper,
Hello buddy "How are you".

Handshake

Friendship must be nurtured,

Even watered with some tears.

Its roots so strong

And run so deep

To last throughout the years.

Riches can be fleeting,

Health can go away.

But the handshake

Of your true best friend,

Will stay

And stay

And stay.

Far From The Crowd

Far from the crowd I'd like to be,

Alone with you, just you and me.

Hands held tightly we'd walk along,

Listen to the music

Of our two hearts in song.

It would be so easy

To find things we love to do,

For we would be together

Alone—just me and you.

Mom And Dad

Your hands are rough and rugged,
Deep wrinkles line your brow,
Your hair has turned to silver grey,
Your heads are slightly bowed.
You walk with the hint of a shuffle,
From countless steps of years gone by,
But we hear no words of sorrow,
Only that those years did fly.
Your touch is still like velvet,
Your eyes don't miss a thing,
You stand strong in quiet waiting,
For the good things life can bring.
Your smile is quick in coming,
Spreading to a big ole grin,
When the fruits of all your labor
Ring your doorbell and come in.
I know each wrinkle very well
For I helped put them there,
Each day you had to worry,
When I was young and in your care.
I thank God he chose you for my parents
I'm so honored and so glad
So I'll take this time to tell you,
I really love you Mom and Dad.

I'm A Farmer

As I look to the horizon,
I see waves of golden brown.
The wind does softly rustle
From each wheat stem, head on down.
Many days ago I started,
Tilled the earth to catch the rain,
Each seed was sewn and planted,
With much worry and some pain.
I prayed we'd get the moisture
For each seed to sprout and grow,
To reach this day of harvest
Though I really did not know.
You see Lord-I take chances,
I'm a farmer and proud to be.
I have looked at other choices,
But this choice was really me.
So I've done within my power
All the work that I can do.
What's left to make this harvest
Depends solely upon you.

My Earth

No where on earth
Is the air so sweet,
As on this land beneath my feet.
Here I am unshackled,
From the chains of life that bind,
My spirit free-not bridled,
My troubles left behind.
I can look to far horizons,
See all that I can see,
But on this land beneath my feet,
My heart will always be.

Beginning

From the beginning
My heart was happy
Just having you around.
Today still brings
The magic of the love
In you I found.

Alone

I've seen the sun, felt the rain,
I'm lost and know not why.
Loneliness beckons with its silent call.
And I cry at being alone.

My land of Memories

I walk my land of memories,
Savor all but just a few.
I can see so many faces
Of friends that I once knew.
The years that total many
are now gone and in my past.
Some names I have forgotten
Some will always last.
I stop and have to chuckle
At some things we use to do,
Oh those memories are so special,
But the times were special too.
I just hope my friends much younger,
Will have memories that always last
And can stop some day and chuckle
At this face from in their past.

Treasures

Treasures sunk on the mighty seas
Lost to time—to always be,
Riches of the years long past,
Gone forever in a lightning flash.
Treasures of the written word
Priced from cheap to the absurd,
Words to read to understand
Their pleasure found in every land.
Treasures hanging on a wall,
Of painted past-a mountain tall.
Scene's of life for all to view,
To visit times to us are new.
Treasures found in mountain sides,
Where gold and silver do abide.
Drill beneath the earthy crust
To find the wells of wealth we must.
Yet the treasure that means most to me
Is in my heart to always be.
Placed with tenderness and utmost care
My love for you is hidden there.

Heavenly Body

A sky full of stars, a moon so big and bright
I feel I can reach out and touch it.
A smile comes to my heart,
For I am holding that heavenly body of yours;
So close and tight to me,
And I am at peace.

Chapters

The chapters of life go on and on,
Some will be short-some will be long.
Some will be happy, some way too sad,
Some will read well, a few will be bad.
You must keep on writing
Those pages of yours,
Keep filling your book
With your life's tours and detours.
Fill all the pages
With things you have done,
Some that you have lost at,
Some that you won.
Some pages will have goodness,
Some pages, some strive.
The last page must stay empty.
For the final page of your life.

Time

Long to arrive, soon to pass,
Memories stolen from time.
Time, my friend,
Long to arrive, it will again.

Future

Into the future we cannot see,
Only the present we all must be.
Be kind to times as they are cast,
Soon they'll be over,
Just part of your past.
Future is something you can plan,
Write them down as soon as you can.
For when your down, low as can be,
Just turn a page and you can see.
Hello tomorrow.

I'm an Island

I feel I am an island,
Surrounded by the sea.
Each day another storm comes by,
Washes waves all over me.
But I stop and smile to heaven,
Thank my God for where I stand,
With him to help me take a step,
I'll put new footsteps in the sand.

An Old House

A house filled full of memories,
Sits over the next small hill,
Seems so long since I've been home
And time has not stood still.
I'll trace again my footsteps,
Of a free and happy time,
When days long in pleasure,
And the evenings sublime.
I'll renew some lovely memories,
That are locked within my mind,
The years will simply melt away,
In those memories I will find.
Some moments I will laugh so hard,
Then maybe shed a tear,
For those memories are a part of me,
Have been so many years.
I'll hear my Mothers laughter,
See my Fathers big old grin,
I'll feel love they both inspire,
In the hugs they give again.
Too short the time I'll spend there,
To rekindle the fire in me.
But oh those lovely memories,
Stay within to always be.

Friendship

I know my friend you're feeling low,
For fate dealt you a mighty blow,
If you feel the need
For this old friend,
No matter time, nor place,
Not even when.
Just call me up, no need to ask,
My hand is here, for you to grasp.

Rainstorm

Clouds rolling in, dark blues and grey,
Hiding the sun and its shining rays.
The air is so still, no birds are in flight,
Just eerie silence, like the darkest of nights.
Lightning is flashing, thunder does roar,
Its not a good time for meeting outdoors.
Wind now is blowing, trees are all bent,
Everyone hopes rains all that's been sent.
Its name has not changed since the day
The day we were born,
All we are having is a summer rainstorm.

Springtime

Winter now completely past,

Spring was late but came at last.

Birds are back, now in pairs,

Buildings homes that are only theirs.

A vast array of colors spread,

From beds of flowers long looked dead.

Finally grass again is green,

Air is sweet or so it seems.

How fine it is this time of year,

Spirits rise, we all cheer.

These months have come and none to soon,

April, May, and finally June.

Long Ago

Long ago I fell in love
With someone I thought she would be,
Today I love her even more
Because I discovered she was.

Happiness

I'm able to greet the morning
Wearing my brightest smile,
To have an aura of serenity
Follow me throughout the day,
My thoughts are calm, my heart at ease,
Because I know as each moment passes
That someone cares.
As good as all this makes me feel,
I know the joy within me is for real,
And all the things I'll ever do,
My happiness comes in loving you.

Feelings

Feelings are hard to put into words,
They lack the intimacy, the excitement,
The warmth you create in me.
They cannot show the joy, the elation,
Or the strength of those feeling
I have for you,
All they can do is try to explain
The love I hold for you inside me.

Cry

My love, my love,
Each day I hear your cry,
Or is it mine?

Sweet Thoughts

Many things I have found,
I cannot do.
One is to let a day go by,
Without sweet thoughts of you.

You

The brightness of your smile,
The sweetness of your lips,
The twinkle of your eyes,
The movement of your hips.
The freshness of your presence,
The creativity of your mind,
The frankness of your opinion,
The laughter you freely find.
These are a few good reasons
I love you like I do,
There is so many others,
Each day there's something new.

Days

Some days are worth the waiting,
Some days are best for dreams,
Some days go slowly by,
Some days won't come it seems.
Some days are quickly gone
When I want for them to stay,
Some days for me are special
Remembered in a special way.
Those are days that we together
Do the things we like to do,
Those are the my days of sunshine
For they were spent with you.

Raindrops of Love

Awakened by the muffled sound
Of raindrops on the roof,
I see pale flecks of light thru
The low hanging clouds overhead.
I listen to your deep, gentle breathing
As you lie beside me
In this warm and cozy bed.
I slowly and quietly reach to touch
And hold your soft hand,
Allowing your love and my security
To flow into me.
Such a wonderful and beautiful way
To start a new and peaceful day.

MOM

I don't remember being on your knee,
Yet I can feel it inside of me,
I can't remember when first we touched,
The last I can—so very much.
I do remember you being there,
To wash my face, to comb my hair.
All the times I asked for aid,
Not once refused, not all repaid.
All the love you gave to me,
I've saved and use it sparingly,
It lifts me when I am down,
Comes to me without a sound.
So even though your far away,
Mom your with me everyday.

JUNE

Months of the year vary in fun
Some we look forward to,
Others just come.
December is Christmas
And its bunch of cheer,
January's not bad,
It starts a new year.
September for kids,
Is away back to school,
March is too windy,
And sometimes too cool.
July is real hot,
August not better,
October, November,
Good football weather.
April and May

Are for new thing to grow,
February sometimes
Brings an end to the snow.
June got to be the best time
Of the year,
School time is over,
Vacations are here.
Its time for family,
Its time for friends,
Reunions and weddings,
The fun never ends.
Swimming and picnics
All over town.
Everyone waits for June
To come around.
Birthdays are special,
Memories are to,
So bring on the good month,
June—we're waiting on you.

Dolphins

If we had been Dolphins,
Swim the deep blue seas,
I know we'd be together,
For you'd be the same as me.
We'd explore the mighty oceans,
Both near and far away,
You'd just be in a Dolphins heart.
As you are in mine today.

Your Love

I have walked the world of rainbows
With Daisy's and Roses around me.
I have enjoyed nights of serene peace
With only the moon and a shining star
To light my way.
I have felt the absolute pleasure
Of sharing a love that has taken me to
Heights no one has reached before.
I discovered a new world, our world,
That consists of only you and I.
I cry with happiness,
At what I have discovered,
For I have felt the tender touch
Of your love

Beautiful

There is nothing more beautiful
Then to look into the eyes
Of someone you love,
And see their love for you,
Looking back.

Love We Now live

With the love I give you freely,
With the love with you I share,
With the love from you that I receive
I've found new ways to care.
A whole new world awaits me
With the love in you I find.
My heart full of contentment
I've gained new piece of mind.
I hope you've found enjoyment
From the love to you I give
I pray this lasts forever
This love that we now live.

Spring

The day is dark and dreary

Rain still slowly fall

Tiny droplets dripping from the ivy on the walls

Leaves are slowly drifting down,

From their summer home above,

It will be a while now before spring can

Show her love.

Winter now is seeking its turn to let us see

The vicious strength it carries,

Yet the pristine beauty it can be.

Though the wind is cold and icy,

Rushing from the far, far north,

I know that spring is coming

In my heart I feel her warmth.

Two Are We

Two are we,
Yet I feel the oneness of us,
In thought, in desire, in need
In feelings
I want the whole world to know
The happiness you have brought to me,
With the beautiful and satisfying feeling,
You give my heart and soul
By loving me.

Dreams

Hold on to your dreams
Don't let them die
Or you'll forever look
And wonder why.
Look to those dreams,
Make them come true
For then you'll know the
Reason why,
Was because of you.

Wonderment

Do butterflies have people
In their stomachs,
When the game is on the line,
Do birds like to listen
To the music we make.
Do turtles think
Snails are slow
Or that we are to fast.
Do flowers love us
The way we do them.
Do stars watch us
With the same wonderment
And amazement we do them,
Do people get just as wet
Running in the rain
As they do by walking.
Is a rainbow as pretty to you
As it is to me.

The Mind

The mind is our window
To the world,
As long as its open
Freshness can come in
Like the newness of a morning,
To close it would just shut out
New ideas,
Just as it will close out the light.
To close it completely, will stifle it
Cause it to become as stagnant and stale
as the air in a closed room.
Let us keep our windows open
And uncovered,
So our minds can breathe and grow.

Dreams

Although we can only live
A day at a time,
We can hold yesterdays memories,
So close in our hearts and mind
And we can dream tomorrows
Dreams,
For they have yet to become reality.

Lament to a whiskey bottle

Maybe from you
I can recall my youth,
Or forget that life has passed me by.
Maybe from you,
I'll find courage
Or recognize my fears.
Maybe from you,
I can be someone else
And forget who I've become.
Maybe in you I'll find strength,
Or find I no longer need it.
Maybe from you,
I'll find I don't have to care,
Or maybe from you I'll realize
And finally see,
You are nothing but an empty
Whiskey bottle and your
Emptiness has emptied me.

Years

The years have come,
Flown swiftly by,
Yet my love for you
Continues to grow.
Today I love you more
Then yesterday
And have the realization
In my heart,
Knowing that I'll love you
Even more tomorrow.

Passing Thru

Have I left a smile
Upon your heart,
Or was I passing thru.
Did I brighten your day
From dawn to dark
Or was I passing thru.
Did I leave a mark
When I was there,
Or was I passing thru
Will you remember
When I am gone,
Or was I passing thru.
Did I give you help
In the best of ways,
Have I really tried
With all I could,
Or was I only passing thru.

Wounded Bird

Pick up gently
This wounded bird,
In your soft and gentle hands,
Heal his broken wings with love
So again with you he'll fly.

Proud American

Into the fiery breech we stand,
To defend, protect
This promised land.
No more insults,
Nor stepped on toes,
Its time for action
Its time for blows.
We've backed down plenty
On things just past,
We can't go further
Or we will not last.
Its time to find out
Where and when,
For these proud and
Determined Americans.

A Smile

Sometimes I feel as though
I can't bear the added weight
Of a feather,
Or the trauma
Of another thought.
Then I stop, remember the
excitement you instill in my life,
The knowledge I am not alone.
I feel the pleasure of those moments
We so lovingly share
And a smile comes to my heart.

The Need

I need your love to raise my spirits whenever
I feel my strength begin to ebb,
To warm me when my body is cold.
I need your love to hold onto
Whenever I'm lost or lonely,
To feed my emotions when they hunger
For your soft and gentle touch.
I need your love to guide me thru
The troubled waters I encounter along the way,
To be my haven, my safe and secure refuge
For all eternity.
I need your love to nurture my dreams and desires
To flow into me each time I need its assurance
I need your love to direct the music that plays in my
in my heart, to orchestrate each melodious word
into a lifetime of song.
I need your love when I need a friend
To bring a smile to my lips and my heart
I need your love to dry my tears
to bring rainbows when my shies are grey
I need your love today
For all the tomorrows yet to come,
To walk each step with me
As we journey through life.
I'll need your love forever and beyond.

Mr. Sun

Welcome to another day
Mr. brightly colored sun,
It seems as only yesterday
At this time your day had begun.
Did you bring again
Your warming rays,
For flowers now in bloom,
Your shining light to brighten up
A dark and lonely room.
Push away those shadows,
That linger from the night,
Bring to light those lovely things
Put them In our sight.
Help make this day a happy one
That your welcome sunshine can,
Hold us gently thru the day
In your warm and sunny hands.

Your Happiness

Whatever o'clock in the morning
Lying here in bed,
Thinking of some special times,
And special words to me you said.
I truly know those moments,
Mean more to me today,
To put them down in simple words,
I hardly know the way.
You would have to feel this fire,
That burns my body thru,
Feel the awesome strength and beauty,
Of this love I have for you.
You would have to see the pictures
I carry in my mind,
Those I hold so dearly,
Took so many years to find.
Can words explain the feelings
Deep within my heart and soul,
In my thoughts, my dreams,
My wishes
Of those memories I do hold.
I want you to be happy
For that was meant to be,
I hope the happiness that you find,
You will always find with me.

Son

You've made the wisest choice
That—I plainly see,
For the life you lead
Is yours to live,
Not to live for me.
The feelings held inside my heart
Are hope and love and pride,
For what you did, you did for you
And what you felt inside.
Don't regret your wise decision,
As the years begin their toll,
For doubts will always seem to come,
When you have gotten old.
So start today to forge ahead,
In what you chose to do,
For only God in heaven knows
The path he chose for you.

We are We

Could you feel my heartbeat quicken
As you whispered in my ear.
Could you feel my arms around you
Even though I wasn't near.
Could you see the love light shining
From eyes that held some tears
As you softly and so gently
Calmed and soothed my biggest fears
Could you hear the words
I whispered
As I held you close to me
Darling I so love you,
I'm so happy we are we

Leaves

I hope someday to finally see
Someone solve this mystery
With some training and a lot
Of luck
That leaves on trees
Instead of down
Learn the art of falling up.

Morning

Morning crisp from cold night air
Mist slowing rising to the sky from
Dark quiet waters of ponds sprinkled
Across the rolling landscape.
Each blade of grass glistens
From the light of a morning sky,
As they stand like soldiers
At attention from the frost
That covers them.
Mother nature has painted
Another temporary picture
For us to enjoy,
As another day begins anew.

Spring

The day is dark and dreary
Rain still slowly falls
Tiny droplets dripping
From the ivy on the walls.
Leaves are slowly drifting
From their summer home above,
It will be awhile before spring
Can send her love.
Winter now is seeking
Its turn to let us see,
The vicious strength it can carry,
The pristine beauty it can be.
Though the wind is cold and icy
Rushing from the far, far north,
I know that spring is coming
In my heart I feel her warmth.

Beginning

From the beginning
My heart was happy
Just having you around.
Today still brings the magic,
Of the love in you
I found.

My Love

My love, my love,
Listen to the words
My heart is speaking.
Feel the feelings
I hold inside.
Catch and hold my soft caress
My tender kiss.
See who's image
Is in my eyes.
Who's love I hold and treasure
In my heart and soul.
You know her well my love
For she is you.

You

I want to see, to smell
To taste, to feel
To reach to hold, to love
You.

My Strength

This light I see,
Is it from the moon
Or from the fire that burns
In my heart and soul
The air is chilled but I feel the
Warmth of your love thru out
My body.
My mind races from one place
To another,
As I remember all and everything
We've done to please and satisfy
This lovely, yet demanding love
I have for you.
I feel weak, yet my strength is greater
Then I have known before because
I draw from yours.
I need the security, the place I can
Escape my worries and relax
With peaceful thoughts.
I feel so good already
Because I know that all I have to do
Is come home to you.

I Can Only Give

I can only give you love,
For the peace you've brought to me.
For the smile on my heart,
To my life its harmony.
I can only give you love,
For accepting me as I am,
For the times that we embrace,
For the comfort you have been.
I can only give you love,
For the time you've been my friend,
For the joy you've give to me,
For this love that will not end
I can only give you love

Because

Because of and thru you
My shining star,
I found out who I am
And can be.

Tomorrows

There will never come a day,
I won/t think lovely thoughts of you,
When I won/t feel your magic touch
Or see the smile that warms me.
There will never come a day,
When your shining eyes
Won/t melt away my troubles,
And leave me in a peaceful,
Serene world
The sharing of oneself
You have instilled in me
Are feelings I want to share with you
Today and all our tomorrows.

Today

The ability, the opportunity,
To build a relationship,
Is known by so very few.
The depth of our love,
The strength of our feelings,
The incomparable heights of joy,
Only make me realize all this has
Just begun
And I will have a lifetime to grow,
Become closer to you.
This I promise starting with today.

Gods Rose

A flower blooms, its petals frail,
Its colors defined in great detail.
Its sweet aroma I feel, I smell
In a heart filled with love
To always dwell.
In my garden of life you/ll always be
My prize blue ribbon, my ecstasy,
For of the millions of flowers
Gods garden grows,
I get to love his finest rose.

Thanksgiving

On this special day, this time of year
I'd like a moment to let you hear,
I thank you for my darling wife,
I thank you for my extra life,
I thank you for my every son,
I thank you for the friends that come,
I thank you for this food we see,
I thank you God for loving me.

American Eagle

Soar freely skyward mighty eagle,
Ride the thermals high,
Fight to live majestic bird,
Spread your wings and fly.
You are this country's symbol,
Of freedom for us all,
Our strength and bravest courage,
Our right to stand so tall.
May you always keep on flying,
For all of us to see,
America/s Eagle, you've earned the right,
To fly, so high, so free.

American soldier

I hear the rolling thunder
Of the cannons mighty roar,
I see my comrades falling all around me
By the score.
I will not break, nor waver,
Nor hide or start to run
As this deadly fight for freedom
Is one that must be won.
The right to choose our pathway,
Must be held and be preserved.
For this and the rights of others,
I'll fight and proudly serve.
My beliefs are strong and solid.
I stand here and will not bend.
I will fight this fight forever,
Or to its bitter end.

My Love

Thank you my love for the words you say,
That fill my heart and make my day.
Thank you my love for what you do,
And for all the reasons I love you.
Thank you my love.

Alone In
A Crowded Room

A candle lit and burning bright,
Yet overpowered by your radiance.
We dine alone, oblivious to this crowded room.
A glass of wine
A toast for two,
Knowing you feel our love
The way I do.
I taste the sweetness of you tender lips
And drink again from the nectar of your kiss
While I absorb more of the magic you use
To make my days so memorable.

You

Its been thru you my love,
I have found some precious moments.
You have stilled the cry of loneliness
That echoed loudly throughout the
Inner chambers of my soul.
You have brought sunshine for my days,
Starlight for my nights,
Your light for my dreams.

Pathway To Happiness

Must my days be filled with this struggle
Inside me
Can not this loneliness subside.
I only want this love I have for you
To grow forever.
I want the world to know that
Dreams can come true.
I have felt the softness of your
Hand in mine and have lost myself
Forever in the paradise of your arms.
I have walked the pathway of happiness
With you at my side,
You have rescued me from the abyss
Of loneliness and held me safe and secure
With just your kiss.

Sun Slowly Setting

My sun is slowly setting into the horizon,
I can feel my spirit ebb,
I find myself dwelling upon the pleasant
And sweet memories that are such a wonderful
Part of my life.
I wonder if I have accomplished even a small
Part of the dreams I dreamed in my youth.
I smile as I remember a dream or wish
That somewhere and sometime along my way
Has come true.
Yet I find that tears come easily for I realize
That some will never be fulfilled.
I so wish I could have seen some things earlier
In life the way I see them today,
For that would have given so much more time
To enjoy them.

I Feel

I feel like a candle unlit would feel
If it could,
A song with beautiful words
Yet has no music.
A star with no twinkle,
A shore without a sea.
For you have gone,
Taken some of me with you
Yet happiness fills me,
For I know I have more of you
In return.

Yours

I'm yours for all your dreams,
For the times you are lonely
The times you want someone
With you to watch the stars.
For the times you need to smile
Or laugh.
For the times you need someone
To lean on,
For the times you need love
Whispered in your ear.
I'm yours,
Whenever.

Wedding Prayer

Our heavenly father
Today we embark on a journey
We pray will never end.
We know and understand there will
Be mountains for us to climb,
That the road ahead may not be paved
All the way.
But together with you to lead us,
We can and will overcome any obstacles,
Life may put in our way.
May our days be filled with sunshine,
Our nights serene and cloudless,
With the stars and your heavenly love
As our secure and warm blanket.
With your love-our love will prevail
Thru difficult times.
Our lives will be enriched,
As we grow together.
We thank you God for giving us this chance,
To begin this journey as one.

Stupid Ball

Darkness is closing in around me,
My friends have gone their separate ways.
Leaving me alone in my solitary quest
With only the creatures of the night
As company.
But I know I can, I know I must,
Make this stupid little putt
Before I get my rest.

The Years

The years have come and gone,
Flown so swiftly by,
Yet my love for you continues
To grow.
For today I love you more
Then yesterday,
And the realization in my heart
That I'll love you even more—
Tomorrow.

The Windmill

A windmill standing like a sentinel
Of the prairie,
Drawing the life giving water from
Deep below the sod of this gentle
Rolling grassland.
I can sit at the top and see forever.
All the birds of the air
And the animals of the area seem to
Find their way to the sweet fresh
Water that overflows this stock tank.
Such a calm and peaceful place
To sit and dream about what the
Future holds.
Just a plain old windmill to most
But a haven to dream my dreams
Of tomorrow.

My Friend

A friend who listens
When I am blue,
A friend who cares
Because I need her to.
A friend who loves me every day,
In such a sweet and unashamed way.
A friend who brings the joy to my life
So lucky am I for she is my wife.

A Day at A Time

Although we can only live
One day at a time,
We can hold on to yesterdays memories
In our heart and soul
And we can dream tomorrows dreams
For they have yet to become reality.

Kansas

Waves of golden heads of grain
Gently rolling before a southern breeze.
The fresh distinct smell of newly mown hay
Is in the air.
Far in the distance trees outline a river
As it slowly winds its way
Across the level plains.
Farms—Alive with their dedicated
Hard working people
Dot the landscape.
Swirls of dust rise intermittently
From the fertile land we know
As the heart of the world,
The beautiful and peaceful land
That will always hold a special place
In my heart.
Kansas—My Kansas—My home.

Goals

These are the days of futures past
When we look at dreams,
Are they true at last.
Have we done all what we hoped to do
Or have you in truth disappointed you.
Life does not treat us all the same
But the chance to improve will always remain.
Without the desire, a hope or a care,
Our cupboard of dreams will still be bare.
So take a glance, No—a real hard look,
Have we reached the goals in our life's book,
If not, the things left for us to do,
Those goals to reach are up to you.

Our Tomorrows

On the coldest of days
I feel the warmth of your love
And wonder why all our yesterdays
Could not have been as sweet
As we have made our tomorrows.

I Dream Dreams

I dream dreams of dungeons deep
With chains and shackles
Around my feet,
To escape in time my quest to meet
The need to save my princess sweet.
I dream dreams of mountains high,
That go on and on
Touch the sky,
Yet I'd climb and climb
Thru all the pain
Just to hear your whispered name.
I dream dreams of oceans deep
I sail the waves from my captains seat
To keep a long awaited date
With a special love
My treasured mate.
I dream dreams.

Dad

You've always stood there Dad,

So strong, so straight, so tall,

You've been our rock to lean on,

Not just one, but to us all.

Some of your strength we're meeting

After all these many years

Thru all the heartaches that we caused you,

And yes-some big ole tears.

We hope we've made you proud

As proud as you can be

That the job you did to raise us,

Bore fruit the world can see.

The best thanks that we can give you,

As we pass the parent test,

Is to say you've been so good for us

Thank God Dad-you've been the best.

From Afar

Have you ever felt someone's heartbeat
From afar,
I have—yours
Have you tasted someone's lips
Though the miles apart
Forbid an actual touch,
I have—yours
Have you ever placed a kiss
On someone's heart,
Yes-you have—Mine.

Your Footprints

I have followed footprints in my path
Of persons I have met,
Just to reach a point in life
A place I wished I/d get,
Now I've passed the years of golden youth
I'm wiser in many ways,
The many footprints I have placed,
Are being covered every day.
But the footprints that you placed within my heart,
They will not go away,
I caress and hold them safely there
I touch them every day,
I now know each step I took
And the ones that will be new
Can never touch the steps I took
In forever loving you.

Beneath My Feet

No where on earth is the air so sweet
As on this land beneath my feet.
Here I am unshackled
From the chains of life that bind,
My spirit free, not bridled
My troubles left behind
I can look to far horizons
See all that I can see,
But on this land
Beneath my feet,
My heart and soul will be.

Rivers

Rivers belong where they can rumble
Eagles belong where they can fly,
You belong in my arms,
More as the days go by.

Golden Years

My years have turned to golden
My eyes have grown dim,
My hair has turned to silver gray
And getting sorta thin.
My feet still have the music
But my legs have lost the beat,
I still can/t stand the icy cold,
And its hard to bear the heat.
The only thing still going
Has not changed in all the years.
My love for you keeps growing
Our memories still bring cheers.
Its not hard to keep on going,
For the past I'll always see,
The future still brings happiness
As you walk each step with me.
So although my years turned golden
And my eyes have grown dim,
My heart is full and happy
As my life with you has been.

My Star

My Star, My Star
My shining star
You're so close
And yet so far.
I often wonder how you are
My star, my star, my shining star.

Years To Love

The years have come and gone
Flown so swiftly by
Yet my love for you
Continues to grow,
I love you more today then yesterday,
And know in my heart,
That I'll love you more tomorrow.

I Love You

I remember our first caress
Our first embrace, that tender kiss,
I remember the sparks that flew
When first we touched
When first we knew.
I remember as time goes by
Each word we spoke, each big sigh
I hear them now in all I do,
In those magic words of
I love you.

Ventures

Some never venture to distant skies,

Others do but do not see

Some have dreams,

Then will not try.

Others loves, that never die.

I ventured

I loved,

Now wonder why

How could I be such a lucky guy.

Sweet Memories

So long to arrive, so soon to pass,

Now sweet memories

Stolen from time.

Time, my dear friend

So long to arrive

And it shall again.

A Memory

Time seems to find a way to carry out
Its endless quest to pass us by
With hardly a heartbeats wait for us
To savor its precious moments.
But time can never erase a memory,
For once we've locked it in our heart and soul,
Time can not find a way to take it away.
No matter how many times we caress it,
Or lovingly hold it
And tenderly tuck it away again,
A memory will remain as precious
As the first time it was put there.

Times

There are times to think about you
There are times to hold you close.
There are times to say I love you
Those are the times I cherish most.
There are times when I am lonely,
There are times I feel so sad,
Those are times to bring back memories
Of the lovely times we had.
There are the times that I am with you
And I want so much to stay,
These are the times I savor
When I have to be away.

Some Never

Some taste victory, yet never are winners

Some lose, yet are never defeated,

Some know the answers

Yet still seek wisdom

Some see the pages,

Yet never the words.

Some look for courage

Yet they are the brave.

Some beg for love,

Yet they are the ones who can give it.

Some cry out for strength

Yet they are the strong.

Remember

Remember how we use to be
All the tomorrows we'd yet to see,
Remember.?
Remember all the times we shared,
And didn't know how much we cared.
Remember?
Remember them-remember this
The days, the months, the years we've missed
Remember?

Paradise

Oh my lady of infinite charms
I love to hold you in my arms
Just to have you hold me tight
Gives my heart so much delight.
When I look into your eyes that shine
Makes me happy that you are mine.
Today, tomorrow the rest of our lives,
We've lived our moments in paradise.

Thank you God

The gentle sound of an evening breeze
Sooths my soul as it whispers thru the trees,
Such a peaceful time I'm glad I'm here
Its brought back memories I hold so dear
I can quietly reflect on the past and to the
Future and where I want to be
So I thank you God for this evening breeze
For my peaceful time
And for all you've done for me.

Friendship

A friendship that has no boundries
To accept each as we are,
Help us to overcome our weaknesses,
Yet strengthen our strongest strengths.
From such an unlimited friendship
We will continue to grow.
But the change will be so subtle
Even the two of us won't know.

Song Keeps Playing

Each time I get to hold you,
How good to me it feels,
Its always like the one at first
And will never lose appeal.
My heart just keeps on dancing,
Our song will always play.
I listen to its melody,
Each day, by day, by day.
Its music is so lovely,
The words are oh so real,
They say how much I love you,
And that's just how I feel.

You

Yes, you are in my thoughts today,
There you are
There you'll stay

My Flower

A flower blooms

Its petals frail,

Colors defined in great detail.

Its sweet aroma, I feel, I smell,

In a heart filled with love

To always dwell.

You'll always be my prize blue ribbon,

My ecstasy.

For the millions of flowers,

Only God can grow,

I get to love his finest rose.

My Garden

My garden started long ago

In it Gods finest rose did grow,

Years went by, time it flew,

Then God blessed me

With rose number two.

Now again today, my garden grew,

My roses no longer add to two,

For in front of all who were there to see,

God gave another rose to me.

Mountains

God made some mountains for us to climb,

Gave us days not too sublime,

But he gave us wisdom for us to see,

And the strength to be strong,

When we must be.

So we carry on, our hopes still high

To surpass those days we wonder how and why

We just must stop, and thank him for,

The things we have, the people we adore,

We have our kids, their children too,

So really no reason for us to be blue,

So today I'll try hard to stand up tall,

For I know you're there in case I fall

I'll wear a smile, be glad at heart,

For it's a brand new day,

His Trust

My life now full of rainbows,
Its seen the last of rain.
For now we are together
And share the same last name.
We'll be together always
In the years yet left to come,
To share our love, to share our life
And feel as though we're one.
I thank you for this feeling,
I have inside me every day,
You've made me oh so happy,
I love you in every way.
God has sent a special angel,
To fill my heart with love,
I promise each day to honor
His trust from up above.

Three Of The Best

This moment is to savor
To remember for all time,
For the person standing on that stage,
Is truly ours, yours and mine
Many have worked to help him,
To achieve all he has done,
Its great to see a victory,
Especially one won by a son.
I only wish that special someone,
Could have seen him take that walk,
For he believed in youngsters,
Who would work and not just talk,
I can feel emotion rising,
Thru my body to my chest,
Oh Mother of our youngest child,
Now there's three that are the best.

Agony

The agony and pain inside me
So heavy to endure,
How can I go on with this burden I bear.
All I hear is a crushing silence,
Even words I cry aloud have no sound.
Is there no one to hear my plea
Or am I doomed to live with these feelings
That struggle so hard to escape.
To be heard, to be felt,
To be understood,
To be wanted.

Memories

Through memories we revisit times in our life

That make us happy.

Where time does not move,

But stands forever still

And although we're sad to see time pass,

We really shouldn't be.

For time is not the end of memories,

Only a beginning

And we should smile at the joy

The memories created today will bring.

My Soul Touched

You reached out and touched my soul
Again today
I felt your love overpower me once more.
And I settled back into our world,
A world that consists of only you and I.
I am again tranquil, surrounded by your love,
My thoughts and heart racing ahead
To the next time I reach again for my link to
You.
I feel so close to you and curl myself next to
You,
To warm myself in the safe haven
Of your arms and your love.

What You Gave To Me

I've tried hard to explain
Just how I feel inside, about all the happiness
And the joy I hold, but my words are so
Inadequate, so most remains untold.
I truly hope you understand
What I tried so hard to say,
You have made me oh so happy,
It will last me all my days.
You have given to me your tenderness
Your love in all I do.
But the greatest gift you've given
To me you've given you.

Linger Long

Linger long these thoughts of you
Forever stay with me.
Linger long these words I hear
Happy they've made me be.
Linger long these feelings felt,
Within my heart and soul
Linger long this love for you
And will forever hold.
Linger long my shining star
Linger long.

Shoes

Shoes are made with special care,

For on someone's foot they're put to wear,

So many styles from which to pick'

If they don't sell I'll sure be sick.

All these shoes displayed so neat,

But I sure do wish

They were on someone's feet.

I Want

I want, I need you as you are
To have, to hold in futures far.
Please don't change
The things you do,
I love the whole
Not part of you

With Me

If I count all my thoughts
The desires, the feelings, the memories
I keep within.
You're only with me
In everything I do.

Deep Within My Heart

Deep within my heard and soul,

I have more love then I thought could exist,

You have brought to me throughout the years,

More happiness and joy

Then I am entitled to.

So if ever you look for something

You feel I really want

Just give me a reminder

That I have you,

And that my shining star

Is all I'll ever need.

My Love To You

If I only had the power
To make all your dreams come true,
I would so gladly do it,
For someone sweet as you.
If I could fill your world with rainbows,
As far as you could see,
If that would make you happy,
Then happy you would be.
But the only power within me
Is a will, a want, and a way,
And that's to give to you forever,
My love to you each day.

My Peace

I found a piece within me,
That I didn't know before;
Given by a loved one who I treasure and adore,
You gave to me a happiness
That only I can know.
No way can I define it,
I just can let it show.
My heart is so full of love
That I can plainly see
I only hope I've been to you,
What you have been to me.
You have been my sunshine
On many rainy days,
You're always there when needed
In your usual lovely ways.
So I thank you for the greatest gift
That you could give to me
A love to last forever that's made me happy
As I can be,
I know this deep within me
You were sent from up above
To share my life, to share with me
Our deep and precious love

Thank You My Love

Thank you my love for what you say,

You fill my heart

You make my day,

Thank you my love

For what you do

And for all the reasons

I love you.

Alone

Alone, and yet I'm not,
For you are with me in everything I do
I'm alone and lonely,
But know I shouldn't be
For wherever I am you are also
A memory is there each way I turn,
Something to remind me of you
And all you mean to me
The moon, the stars, clouds and rain
Sunshine and rainbows, stars at night,
A word, a laugh, a smile,
And the twinkle in your eyes,
A song on the radio,
All the love in my heart.
And I succumb to the warm and tender
Feeling of our love that overwhelms me,
Then my heart smiles and I no longer
Am alone and lonely—
Just missing you.

Contentment

I see your love shining
From your eyes of liquid light,
I feel your love flowing into me this very night,
I sense the deep felt meaning,
Of our each unspoken word.
Because we each know what we're saying,
Even though no words are heard.
A contentment is within us
As our fingers trace so light,
Those magic places that they roam
That need only touch, not sight.
We know to make us happy
Is as easy as can be,
For all it takes our love to flow,
Is for you to be with me.

Loneliness

Loneliness lies beneath my breast,
Deep within my heart,
I cry out your name and only hear it echo
Through my soul.
I need so much your tender touch,
Your loving arms, your sweet embrace.
I want to again experience the softness
Of your lips on mine,
And smell the fragrant aroma of your hair,
As we lie together in our world of contentment
And love.
I need to hear those unspoken words we find
No need to say,
Because we feel them in our heart.
Oh my lovely angel, again I call your name
Once again I hear it echo,
And I cry at the emptiness and loneliness
I feel inside me.

A Mighty Mountain

As strong as a mighty mountain,

As deep as the deepest sea,

There's just no way of taking back

My love for you from me.

I've had a taste of heaven,

Who I found I deeply love,

You are a special angel,

Sent to me from up above.

I love your every beauty,

All your feelings, all your cares

My love of life is growing

Of that I am aware.

You've instilled in me such happiness

Not found in me before,

You've caused my heart to sing a song

And to great heights to soar,

Thank you my special angel for the love

You gave to me

To treasure, to hold dearly

In my heart to always be.

Days And Hours

Days so long, slow to come
Has time stood still
Refused to run.
Days aren't even, that I know
For some have hours
That just don't show.

Merry Christmas

Merry Christmas to you Mom and Dad,
From one who loves you so,
I wish you both the best of health,
For the years still left to go.
My hope is that you realize and you
Can plainly see,
All the love, the pride, the satisfaction
In the choice of parents God chose for me,
Your guidance, care, and assurance,
Helped smooth the path I took,
The curves, the hills, the valleys,
Became safer under your watchful look,
So thanks to you both Mom and Dad,
For all that you have done,
No matter what's in store on down the road,
Thru the love you shared,-I've won.

Each Passing Day

We've shared a tender moment,
And shared a secret thought,
We've shared a precious moment,
And the peace to each we've brought.
We've shared a morning sunrise
And shared a moonlit sky,
We've shared with each other
Our deepest love,
Never ever asking why.
We've shared plans for tomorrow
We've shared our yesterdays,
We'll share our time forever,
Each day by passing day.

The Smile

I'm sitting alone with dreams of you,
And loving the smile you've just
Put on my heart.

Only Give You Love

I can only give you love for the peace you've
Brought to me,
For the smile on my heart, to my life
Its harmony.
I can only give you love for accepting me as I am,
For the times we have embraced,
For the comfort you have been.
I can only give you love for the time
You've been my friend
For the enjoyment you've gave to me,
For the love that will not end.
I can only give you love.

Life is Just Not Fair

Many times I want to touch you,
But find you're just not there,
Those are the times I'm feeling lonely,
And that life is just not fair.
But then I start to thinking
And it comes back to me,
I really am a lucky guy
That I should plainly see,
You fit so smoothly in my life,
An important part you are,
So I sit back and count my blessings
For the life we shared so far.

I Am Lucky

Truly I am lucky, Blessed by God
Beyond my due,
And in counting all my blessings
Number one would start with you.
I would have to count my children,
The girls they chose for wives
And their kids will be my crown of crowns
I could wear through out my life.
Another blessing is the Mom and Dad,
God picked and chose for me
For without their love to guide me,
I've no idea where I'd be.
So truly I am lucky, blessed by God
Beyond my due
But in counting all my blessings
They would start and end with you.

There Are Times

There are times I ask too much from you
Or it seems that way to me,
But those are the times I so need your strength.
There are times I feel the world closing in on me,
Those are the times I need you to hold me close
So I can be in the comfort of your arms.
There are times when I'm down and feeling blue
Those are the times when I draw upon your
Love to steady me
Until I can stand alone again
I know my love there are times
I ask to much from you but those are the times
I need you so much.

Unspoken Words

Hands held gently, yet as powerful as the bond

That was formed by a kiss that burned deeply

Into my heart and soul.

Unspoken words, yet understood because we each knew what was being said.

A mist of happiness cover my closed eyes

That still can see the moment love found a

Pathway between you and I,

And I hold you close in a world all our own.

Inspiration

The dance floor beckoned as their song played,
Two people in love to their music they swayed,
Just so at ease, so comfortable again'
Its been that way since their love begin.
She fits so smoothly as he holds her tight,
His precious angel, his hearts delight.
A love no longer needing confirmation,
For he had found his inspiration.

Making Memories

There will never be a day when my heart won't smile each time I think of you,
There will never be a day I won't think of a
Tender moment or feel your soft and gentle
Touch,
There will never be a day when I can't picture
Your mischievous grin or see the sparkle
In your eyes,
I found out long ago my life needed you
And it feels so good to know that you'll
Never stop making my memories.

Long To Arrive

So long to arrive, so soon to pass,

Now only sweet memories

Stolen from time,

Time my friend,

So long to arrive,

But it will again.

Hope

Hope is something we all share,

To find a cause in which we care

Something not born, but is instilled,

For us to live our lives fulfilled,

Our parents, our teachers,

You and I must,

Find something together

In which we trust

For as things are going,

Today all around,

Tomorrows won't have a chance to rebound.

So Very Dear

Love is more than just a word,

Not one just read, or one just heard,

It something felt way deep inside,

With one you've laughed,

With one you cried.

An emptiness felt when she's not near,

The one you hold so very dear.

Where You Belong

Rivers belong where they can rumble,

Eagles where they can fly,

You belong in my arms,

More as the days go by.

Fond Memories

Paint a picture in your mind
Of fond memories left behind,
Think of those which lie beyond,
That slowly will come with
Tomorrows dawn.
Paint them pretty with colors bright,
Think of them with sheer delight,
For pictures painted with loving care,
Will be there tomorrow for us to share.

Not Here

My heart cries out, is there no sound,
Am I the only one to hear the cries I feel.
The pain yet I see no open wound,
But this pain will disappear as it
Has before.
Loneliness surrounds me, my dear,
But it only happens when I'm not there
Or your not here.

Dream On

Dream on, dream on my shining star,
Tonight together
We'll await the dawn.

Tears

Tears have dimmed my vision,
An ache has filled my heart
Apart, the pain of loving
Continues from dawn to dark.
This feeling of lonely sadness
I feel so deep inside,
The tears I've shed are not for me,
It's for you I've cried.

Shared Time

Time is shared in all I do,

Some alone-some with you,

The time together went way to fast,

But memories gained

Make those moments last.

This time alone can still be fun

For its time I reflect on all we've done.

Time together-now so few

But time apart still shared with you.

Once Again

I want to see, to smell, to taste, to feel,
To reach, to touch, to hold
You once again.

Just Can't Do

Many things I found
I just can't do.
One is to let a day go by
Without sweet thoughts of you.

I Need You

There are times I ask too much from you,

It seems that way to me,

But those are the times I need your strength.

There are times I feel the world closing in around me,

Those are the times I need you to hold me close

Let me feel the comfort of your arms.

There are times when I'm down and lonely

Those times I draw upon your love to lift me up

To steady me,

Until I can stand alone again.

I know my love there are times I ask too much

From you.

But those are the times I need you so much.

Love Is Good

Is it magic that makes my heart beat with joy,

Each time I hear your voice,

Or is it your love I hear.

Is it just my imagination that I feel with you,

Each and every moment of each and every day,

Or is it your love I feel.

Is it happiness that makes my arms want and need the security of you in them,

Or is it your love that I need and want so much.

You fit so nicely into a pocket of my heart,

How could love like this,

Be anything but good.

Your Light

Its been thru you, my love
I have found many of my life's
Precious moments.
You have stilled the cry of loneliness
That echoed loudly throughout the inner
Chambers of my soul.
You brought sunshine to my days
Peace to my nights
And your light to lead my way.

Remember

Remember how we use to be,
All the tomorrows we'd yet to see
Remember
Remember all the times we shared
Didn't know how much we cared,
Remember
Remember them, remember this,
The days, the months, the years we missed
Remember.

Some Memories

Memories deep within my mind
Some not good but some so fine.
Of friends I had not here today,
Their memories sweet in my mind
Do lay
Of long, long ago when growing up,
Of holstein calves, our ugly pup.
Of football games and touchdown drives,
Some which failed, in all we tried.
Of a miserable day in a bed I laid,
And a friend told me don't be afraid,
Of Mom and Dad are they alright
Sure wish I had them in my sight.
Our wedding day, how far we've come,
Of hard, hard times and yet we won.
Of those three days past, our sons
Were born and kept my life
From being forlorn.
Of friends I hold so very dear,
Some so far, some right here
Of memories fresh, of some so old
But all I keep to have and hold.

Your Mark

In everyone's life someone enter's
Who will leave a mark on you
That even time can not erase,
I have been that lucky person
To have met you.
You left your mark on my heart,
A mark of love,
A love that has been so good to me,
A love so very special because
It was given in love.

Life

We have but just a moment
In the scheme of things called life,
So we must take advantage
Of the love and not the strife.
We can not lose the chances
To be happy while we're here,
Love is the only answer
For the ones we hold so dear.
Life can go so swiftly
In a moment—so we hear.
One day they are among us,
Next day they're just not here
So heed the feelings
In your heart,
Don't ever let them go.
For the love we have within us
Please don't hide it—let it show.

Yesterdays Memories

Yesterdays memories tucked lovingly away

In my heart,

Tomorrows dreams are yet to come.

Will one find its way

To a corner of my heart

and become yet another

Of yesterdays dreams.

Anniversary Memory

Many, many moments have passed
Throughout the years,
The highs and lows of memories
Of some trials and some tears.
Today's another moment
A highlight in my life
For today so many years ago
You said "I Do" and became my wife.

My Wife

In the course of my lifetime
There has been some rainy days
Others filled with love and sunshine
The clouds all stayed away.
My rainy days are over
Sunshine's in my heart for life
It keeps warm the love I carry
For you my darling wife.

My Rainbow

You are to me a flower in spring

Because of all the joy you bring

A bright colored rainbow

With its pot of gold

Because you share this love we hold

Every heavenly star that shines so bright

Because they led me to you

With their guiding light

An angel for me to have and hold

To love forever and never get old.

Special One

In everyone's life someone enters
Leave such a mark even time can't erase
I have been that lucky person
To have met you.
Your mark has been left on my heart
A mark of love
A love that has been so good for me
One that is even more special
Because it was given in love.

Paradise

Oh my lady of infinite charm
I love to hold you in my arms
Just to have you hold me tight
Fills my heart with such delight
When I look into your eyes that shine
Makes me so glad that you are mine
Today, tomorrow, the rest of our lives
We've had our moment—In Paradise.

I'll come running

If ever you need someone to hold you
Just call my name and I'll be there
If ever you're feeling lonely
Remember that someone who cares
If ever you need a day of sunshine
I'll give you one like we shared before
If ever you need a friend
I'll come running
I'll come running until I can't run no more.

Dream Tonight

Hold my hand as we walk alone
Think my thoughts while reading this
Hold me close even though I'm not there
So you can feel just how much I care
Take another piece of my heart
To go with what you've had from the start
Dream with me as you sleep tonight
You'll always be a part of me
And it feels so right.